Contents

Any words appearing in bold, **like this**, are explained in the Glossary.

Scotland

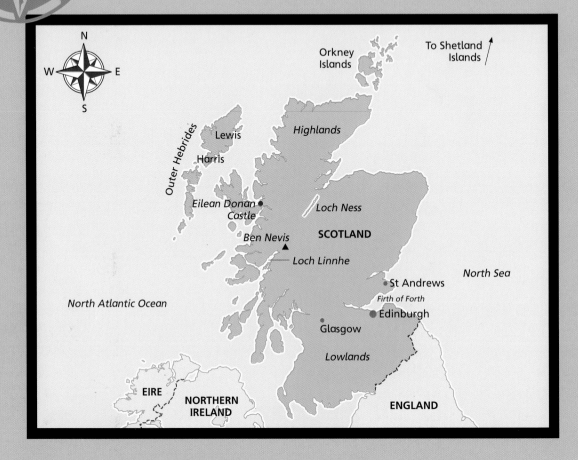

Scotland is a country in the United Kingdom. It is also part of a group of islands called the British Isles. About 5 million people live in Scotland.

The **capital** city of Scotland is called
Edinburgh. Edinburgh has many old
buildings. Edinburgh Castle stands
on top of a hill, looking down over
the city below.

Land

Scotland is a very beautiful country. In the south, there are gentle hills covered with forests and fields. This part of the country is called the **Lowlands**.

The north and west of Scotland is called the **Highlands**. There are mountains, lakes called **lochs** and valleys called glens. Off the west coast, there are hundreds of islands.

Landmarks

The Forth Railway Bridge carries trains over a wide stretch of seawater called the Firth of Forth. This famous bridge is more than 100 years old.

Scotland has many spectacular castles. This is Eilean Donan Castle in the **Highlands**. It stands on an island in the sea. People still live in this castle.

Homes

Scottish people are called Scots. Most Scots live in Edinburgh, Glasgow and other towns and cities in the **Lowlands**. Many live in blocks of flats in the cities.

People in the **Highlands** usually live in small villages. They can be a long way from the nearest town. Farmers used to live in **traditional** houses called crofts.

Food

There are plenty of fish in Scotland's rivers. Among them are salmon and trout, which are delicious to eat. Fish-farmers raise fish in farms on the **coast**.

Haggis is probably Scotland's most famous food. It is made of sheep's **innards** and oatmeal. Scots **traditionally** eat it with neeps (swedes) and tatties (potatoes), or nowadays chips.

Clothes

Young people in Scotland wear comfortable clothes, such as T-shirts, jeans and sports clothes at home or when they play with friends. Many children wear **uniforms** at school.

These men are wearing **traditional** Scottish **kilts**. They are made from tartan, a woollen cloth made in Scotland. Many Scottish families have their own tartan pattern.

Work

There is a lot of oil under the sea off Scotland's east **coast**. People live and work on oil **rigs** in the North Sea, pumping up the oil.

Many people in the **Highlands** and on
the Scottish islands raise animals or
make things at home. This woman on
the Shetland Islands is **spinning** wool
for sweaters.

Transport

Edinburgh and Glasgow are Scotland's busiest cities. Buses and trains bring many people into the cities to work every morning. Glasgow has an underground railway, too.

On the west coast of Scotland, ferries carry passengers, cars, buses and lorries to the islands and across **lochs**. This small ferry crosses Loch Linnhe.

19

language

Most Scots speak English, but many have their own **accent**. People from Glasgow may sound different from people who live in the **Highlands** when they speak English.

In the Highlands and on the islands of Harris and Lewis, many people speak a language called Gaelic, as well as English. Signs are written in both languages.

School

Scottish children start school when they are four or five. They must go to school until they are sixteen. These children are at school in Edinburgh.

In tiny villages on the Scottish islands,
there may only be a few children.
They go to small schools with only
one or two teachers.

Free time

Golf was first played in Scotland. It is a very popular sport there. There are many golf courses around the country. Children often start playing when they are very young.

Tourists come from all over the world to walk or climb in the Scottish **Highlands**. In winter, the mountains are covered with snow and people ski on them.

Celebrations

Every summer, many Scottish people go to the **Highland** games. They might dance, sing, play **traditional** sports or display things they have made.

Scots celebrate the birth of the Scottish poet Robert Burns with lots of fireworks on Burns Night, 25 January. Many also hold parties on New Year's Eve, which the Scots call Hogmanay.

The Arts

Musicians called pipers play the **traditional** Scottish instrument called the bagpipes. It is hard to play well. Pipe bands often play at special occasions such as weddings.

The Edinburgh International Festival takes place every August. Artists perform plays, music, dance, comedy and poetry all over the city. It is the largest arts **festival** in the world.

Factfile

Name   Scotland is part of the United Kingdom of Great Britain and Northern Ireland.

Capital   The capital city is Edinburgh.

Languages   English and Gaelic are the two official languages of Scotland. About 80,000 people speak Gaelic.

Population   About 5 million people live in Scotland.

Money   In Scotland and all the other countries in the United Kingdom the money is called pounds sterling (£). There are 100 pence in one pound.

Religion   The official Christian church of Scotland is called the Church of Scotland. There are other churches and some people follow other religions.

Products   Scotland produces oil and gas, electronics, chemicals, textiles, timber, barley, food, whiskey and cattle. Tourism is important too.

Scottish Gaelic words you can learn

aon (say: ern)	one
dhà (say: dyarh)	two
trì (say: te-ree)	three
tha (say: haa)	yes
chan eil (say: han-yel)	no
hallo (say: hallo)	hello
mor sin leat (say: mar shin let)	goodbye
tapadh leat (say: tah-pu-let)	thank you

Glossary

accent	way words sound when people say them
capital	most important city in a country
coast	edge of the land where it meets the sea
ferries	ships that carry people and vehicles
festival	celebration, where many events take place
golf course	big, grassy area with holes for hitting golf balls into
Highlands	north and west of Scotland
innards	organs in the body, such as the liver
kilts	woollen skirts worn by men
lochs	lakes
Lowlands	south of Scotland
oil rigs	metal platforms out at sea where people drill for oil
spinning	making wool into thread or yarn that can be knitted or woven
tourists	people who visit places on trips or on holiday
traditional	something that has been done the same way for many years

Index

The Saltire, or Cross of St Andrew, is the flag of Scotland.

32